Mirrors

Emme Thompson

Presentation by *BookLeaf Publishing*

Web: www.bookleafpub.com

E-mail: info@bookleafpub.com

ISBN: 9789357619851

First edition 2022

Reminder

For so long I was broken
Meeting you was a reminder
Of the sun catching my face
The sea salt stuck in my hair
Free falling into the unknown
Tomorrows to look forward to
Yesterdays to let go
Hold my hand and run me through the rain
Bring me to the edge and push me over
Wake me up before you go
To the beautiful things about living
That my heart needed to remember

Something to Dream Of

Curious eyes
Studied me closely
The smirk on your face
Told me your name
Like a riddle to solve
We parted ways
I wondered
If I would see you again
Now I wonder
If you followed me that day
As you walked back into me
Synchronicity
It felt like it was meant to be
Destiny
Like a wish from a dream
Again we were talking
Smiling and blushing
Inviting me back to see you again
Giving me something to dream of

Sunlight Love

The sun has been so warm since I met you
I feel it on my face and it reminds me of your
skin
That touch on my cheek that leaves my pale skin
blush
Oh, how you have kept me warm
With your sunlight over my body
I have soaked you deep into my veins
Absorbed your honey like sticky hot wax
In the sun each morning your warm hands have
found me
Kissing my face gently and making their way
into my heart again
Melting me with the warmth of your love once
more

Waking Up Next to You

Waking up next to you
Wrapped under your arms
Warm between your legs
Wedged beneath your blankets
Wasteful moments I spent
Worshipping you in the
World we made of your
Wooden bed frame
Warmly and gently
Whispering softly in your ear
Would you not let me go?
Watching you breathe
Wind blowing the windows
Water beginning to pour
Weather changing atmosphere
Without pause
Without reason
Wind took your breath
Withdrawing your touch
Woke me from my dream
Waves pulsing through me
Washed you away
Weakness within me
Withstanding the feeling of no longer
Waking up next to you

The Tides of Life

Tears that swell up my face
Leaving a nostalgic taste
Ocean tides of promised lies
Drew you closer each moon rise

The very tides that pull you close
Revealing what I fear the most
Nothingness takes your stay
The tides of life pulled you away

Surrendering to the earth and ocean
Not resisting the flow of motion
I breath you in and I let you go
My feelings are an undertow

Dragging me under they wipe me out
Take your love and leave me drought
Let the storm take my senses
Remove all of my broken lenses

For when the storm has gone and past
I am clean and free at last
Floating gently with the sea
Everything I need to be

Floating Nowhere

Floating nowhere when nowhere is home
A place that I feel safe alone
Drifting weightless in this space
Thinking I could glimpse your face

Emptiness, falling all the way down
Weightlessness that kept me around
Not enough to satisfy my yearning
Urge inside me, inevitably churning

Floating away to find where I belong
The place I have waited for so long
Inside myself where love is growing
Bringing me to inner knowing

Glowing Crosswalks

Glowing crosswalks still hold memories
Dizzy from past ecstasies
Night time spent lost in a dream
Things not being what they seem
Silence that wont drown the sorrow
Better days that come tomorrow
Turn inward and I disappear
Just so I can persevere
Darkness revealing what is real
Showing me what needs to heal

Special

You were special
I was special
We were special, of course
Special to me
Something different to you
Just a detour
To stop for healing
Leave when you're done feeling
Took my light
Left me in darkness
To see all that is hidden within me
To see what makes me special
What made you special
Is something still living deep inside me

Love like Broken Glass

Love like broken glass in my bones
When you have gone and left me alone
Every time an opportunity to break me
Evades the illusion that could maintain me
Back and fourth your mind decides and
Tears me apart from the very inside
It hurts the most when you come back
Waiting gives me an anxiety attack
This time has changed me to the core
Your love trudges through my bones no more

With the Seasons

Your love changes with the seasons
Starts hot in the fall
Burns bright through the winter
Sizzles through the spring
Dwindles in the summer
Burnt out by October
To restart for the winter

A Lesson Learned by the Lack of Another

These times in life
The tides of my soul rise
Darkness inside grows heavy
My light is wounded and vulnerable
I feel empty space inside me
Crushing, dark and overwhelming
Space easily filled
Has been easily emptied
It takes more time
Going inward
Breathing
Filling the emptiness
With everything beautiful
Loving care and understanding
Holding space for yourself
Something I could never teach
A lesson learned by the lack of another

When It's Just Me

When it's just me
No destination
No pictures, no place
No idealization
Nothing left to displace
Raw and broken
Cliché lines like
Words unspoken
Nothing to you
But a reflection
You can't see me
You lack introspection

When it's just me
No outward projections
No body around
No more imperfections
Not even a sound
Soft and healing
Sitting in my heart
Feeling my feelings
With every moment
Each sensation
Brings me closer
Higher elevation

My Heart has Been a Garden

My heart has been a garden
A dry and empty place
In need of nurture and nutrients
My roots cut off from me
Slowly softening the ground
To return life to my soil
With my tears I have watered
With my words I have cultivated
Gently placing my hands
Creating sanctuary with care
Through the changing seasons
The roots of my heart grew
From the soil life emerged
Where it hadn't for so long
And my garden thrived
Flowers growing wildly
Wanderers drawn in by energy
Some even tried to pick me dry
Taking pieces for themselves
But my roots are deep now, healed
My heart has been a garden
A vibrant and lively place
Still it grows

Letting Go

Everything is beginning to fade
Meeting you in the eighth grade
All the little things you'd say
To make me blush and look away
Your innocence that I loved most
And how we got incredibly close
You left a place inside my heart
On the day we had to part
I had to put the rest away
Forever, not another day
The version of you that lived in me beating
Little by little, the memories fleeting
I hope that means you walked away
The piece of you that chose to stay
Maybe together were letting go
Learning to reap what we sew

Still Here

I am still here
In the delicate sequencing
Of every flower
In the silver reflection
Of the ocean's moon
In the streetlights along those roads
That we got so lost
In the blinding essence
Of the brightest light
In the goosebumps given
By the darkest shadow
Outside of myself
I am still existing
Tucked into the darkness
Draped around the light
Stillness of the trees
On a warm summer night

Trying to See Consciously

She paints pictures
In her head
Of the world
At her feet
She uses her eyes
To see in fractals
She uses her ears
Listens to angels
Patterns placed
Numbers speaking
Closing her eyes
Trying to see
Consciously

Gratitude

Every night I talk to the stars and moon
I tell them all that I love in my life
They whisper back the secrets of the universe

Lost Words

I have been here for so long
Silence in my throat
Words trapped deep inside
Cut off from my thoughts
I keep moving forward
Past the cold waves crashing
My breath is all I see
Shivering thoughts through my head
Trembling memories
Deep inside my bones
Droplets falling from the sky
Hands slipping
Away from my neck
Release of my soul
Cleansing of my body
The storm subsiding
The waves calming
Rays of light beyond the obscure
I can see clearly
The silence has lifted from deep inside
Lost words can now find my lips
The tide rises to greet me
It hugs me close
In frigid depth
Once unwelcoming waters

Carrying me peacefully
Current guiding effortlessly

* 9 7 8 9 3 5 7 6 1 9 8 5 1 *